Zion's Camp

by Rick Everett

Signature Books · Salt Lake City · 1994

in memory of
Hermie and Alf

Cover design and photo coloration by Randall Smith Associates

◊ *Zion's Camp* was printed on acid-free paper and meets the permanence of paper requirements of the American National Standard for Information Sciences. This book was composed, printed, and bound in the United States.

98 97 96 95 94   6 5 4 3 2 1

ISBN: 1-56085-064-7

Dear Friend,

If you're looking for a religious tract, this isn't it. Ask for a refund.

If not, you may be relieved to know there's nothing here about the Mormon paramilitary expedition to Missouri in 1834 (the original Zion's Camp). This is about 20th-century Utah, the new Zion, as in Zion's National Park.

Not to be confused with vacationing in the great outdoors; this is strictly urban camp, 1950s - 60s vintage, as in "camping it up"—wrapping yourself in a flag, ironing your hair, and lip-syncing to the Andrews Sisters.

Webster's says that camp is a kind of sensibility or way of looking at the pretense in everyday life. Camp looks at the masks we wear, acknowledges our struggles with fashion and "being cool," accentuates our clumsiness, then roars with laughter.

Detachment helps, which is why I chose the past instead of the present. But , hey, the 1990s can be just as campy. So for a moment don't worry about political correctness. We're not laughing at anyone in particular, we're just laughing . . .

Dare to be different.

Promised Valley II: Return to Jackson County.

In Utah's competitive nanny market, Mary's
forced to moonlight.

This year Dad's winning the Soapbox Derby.

The Song of Solomon always gets
a rise out of 'em.

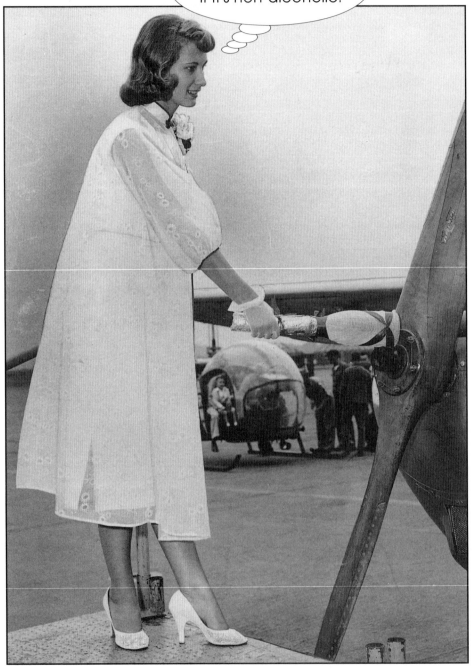

All-WAC Samba finals.

This ward banquet's theme is vegetarian.

Mom's 4 basic food groups: mince <u>meat</u>, <u>fruit</u> pie, <u>bread</u> pudding, and <u>cheese</u> cake.

Temple Marriage.   Wardhouse Wedding.

Not to be outdone—Arthur leaves room for
ten copies of the Book of Mormon.

Only their hairdesser knows for sure.

After threats on the Queen's life,
security is increased at the Gold and Green Ball.

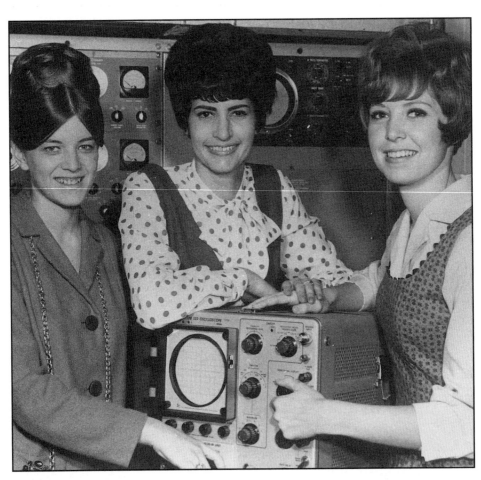

Clever co-eds tune in the Beatles.

Provo mayoral candidate unveils
new campaign posters.

Rachel was taking her "Dear Jane" pretty well.

Famous flames of the Salt Flats.

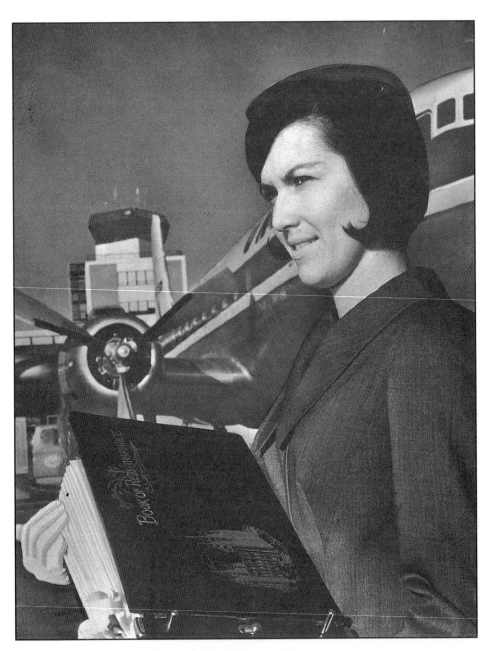

Before Franklin Planners.

Start them young.

The Smith family can hardly wait to see what
Mom's made for dessert.

Pat has decided to lipsync Section 76 for
the ward talent show.

It's obvious who's bucking for
Silver Beaver in this troop.

Still Life with Grapes

The Utah Valley Women's Dramatic Society rehearses its version of *Birth of a Nation.*

"Are you being modest,
or are you just happy to see me?"

ROTC enacts "Don't Ask—
Don't Kiss-and-Tell" policy.

Atomic testing produces strange results
in dorm ChiaPet.

Some must push and some must pull.

Vernal institutes Dinosaur Days.

Miss Utah, her television career in shambles,
hawks her wares outside the temple.

Bishop Hanks is a closet fundamentalist.

Road Kill Show.

Boyz in the 'hood.

How your home teachers know where you are.

Marilyn is clueless.

This Sadie Hawkins Day Race,
Susan wasn't taking any chances.

Phyllis eagerly awaits photographers from
Architectural Digest.

Chuck helps Nan grasp the concept of
"Time and All Eternity."

Sister Jensen poses with her
one-million generation family group sheet.

Viva Las Vacuous!